4❨minute
BIBLE STUDIES

The Power of
Knowing God

Kay Arthur

PRECEPT MINISTRIES INTERNATIONAL

WATERBROOK
PRESS

THE POWER OF KNOWING GOD
PUBLISHED BY WATERBROOK PRESS
12265 Oracle Boulevard, Suite 200
Colorado Springs, Colorado 80921

ISBN 978-0-307-72983-5
ISBN 978-0-307-72984-2 (electronic)

Published in the United States by WaterBrook Multnomah, an imprint of the Crown Publishing Group, a division of Random House Inc., New York.

WATERBROOK and its deer colophon are registered trademarks of Random House Inc.

Printed in the United States of America
2014

10 9 8 7 6

SPECIAL SALES
Most WaterBrook Multnomah books are available at special quantity discounts when purchased in bulk by corporations, organizations, and special-interest groups. Custom imprinting or excerpting can also be done to fit special needs. For information, please e-mail SpecialMarkets@WaterBrookMultnomah.com or call 1-800-603-7051.

CONTENTS

HOW TO USE THIS STUDY

This small-group study is for people who are interested in learning for themselves more about what the Bible says on various subjects, but who have only limited time to meet together. It's ideal, for example, for a lunch group at work, an early morning men's group, a young mothers' group meeting in a home, a Sunday-school class, or even family devotions. (It's also ideal for small groups that typically have longer meeting times—such as evening groups or Saturday morning groups—but want to devote only a portion of their time together to actual study, while reserving the rest for prayer, fellowship, or other activities.)

This book is designed so that all the group's participants will complete each lesson's study activities *at the same time*. Discussing your insights drawn from what God says about the subject reveals exciting, life-impacting truths.

Although it's a group study, you'll need a facilitator to lead the study and keep the discussion moving. (This person's function is *not* that of a lecturer or teacher. However, when this book is used in a Sunday-school class or similar setting, the teacher should feel free to lead more directly and to bring in other insights in addition to those provided in each week's lesson.)

If *you* are your group's facilitator, the leader, here are some helpful points for making your job easier:

- Go through the lesson and mark the text before you lead the group. This will give you increased familiarity with the material and will enable you to facilitate the group with greater ease. It may be easier for you to lead the group through the instructions for marking if you, as a leader, choose a specific color for each symbol you mark.

- As you lead the group, start at the beginning of the text and simply read it aloud in the order it appears in the lesson, including the "insight boxes," which appear throughout. Work through the lesson together, observing and discussing what you learn. As you read the Scripture verses, have the group say aloud the word they are marking in the text.

- The discussion questions are there simply to help you cover the material. As the class moves into the discussion, many times you will find that they will cover the questions on their own. Remember, the discussion questions are there to guide the group through the topic, not to squelch discussion.

- Remember how important it is for people to verbalize their answers and discoveries. This greatly strengthens their personal understanding of each week's lesson. Try to ensure that everyone has plenty of opportunity to contribute to each week's discussions.

- Keep the discussion moving. This may mean spending more time on some parts of the study than on others. If necessary, you should feel free to spread out a lesson over more than one session. However, remember that you don't want to slow the pace too much. It's much better to leave everyone "wanting more" than to have people dropping out because of declining interest.

- If the validity or accuracy of some of the answers seems questionable, you can gently and cheerfully remind the group to stay focused on the truth of the Scriptures. Your object is to learn what the Bible says, not to engage in human philosophy. Simply stick with the Scriptures and give God the opportunity to speak. His Word *is* truth (John 17:17)!

THE POWER OF KNOWING GOD

So much of our confusion and pain, uncertainty and wrong decisions in life come because we do not know God. We may know about Him. We may know what others say about Him. But do we know what God says about Himself? Do we know for ourselves who He really is, how He conducts Himself in the affairs of mankind?

When we know God as He really is, we have a power in our lives, an ability to stand firm. A true understanding of God's character leads not just to knowledge but to action.

> *"The people who know their God will display strength and take action."*
> *(Daniel 11:32)*

Knowing God enables us, as believers, to display strength in times of stress and take action when the rest of the world seems to be immobile.

Through the truths uncovered in this study you will get to know God as never before. In doing so, your strength and faith will increase. You'll be able to stand in confidence, having seen for yourself who your God is, what He wants, and how we can live in relationship with Him.

The Bible—a book God tells us was recorded by man but inspired by Him (2 Timothy 3:16)—begins with God. It ends with God. And everything between the first book of the Bible, Genesis, and the last, Revelation, has to do with God and His relationship with mankind. What an awesome truth, to know that the God of the universe wants to be in relationship with us!

In the sixty-six books that comprise the Bible, you can discover for yourself all God wants you to know about Him, about His ways, and about how you as a human being can have a loving and personal relationship with Him. A relationship that will carry you through any situation, any circumstance of life.

The purpose of *The Power of Knowing God* is to help you see and understand for yourself who God says He is. A personal knowledge of God will enable you to be strong, to stand firm, and to take the action that is needed to handle every situation of life (Daniel 11:32b).

Hang on tight for an eye-opening experience and a lot of interesting discussion as to the practicality of knowing God for who He says He is!

GENESIS 1:1–5

¹ In the beginning God created the heavens and the earth.

² The earth was formless and void, and darkness was over the surface of the deep, and the Spirit of God was moving over the surface of the waters.

³ Then God said, "Let there be light"; and there was light.

⁴ God saw that the light was good; and God separated the light from the darkness.

⁵ God called the light day, and the darkness He called night. And there was evening and there was morning, one day.

OBSERVE

How does God begin the Bible? How does He introduce Himself to mankind in the book that claims to be the very Word of God?

Leader: Read Genesis 1:1–5 aloud. Have the group say aloud and...
- *mark each reference to **God**, including pronouns, with a triangle, like this:* △
- *draw a squiggly line like this* ⌣⌣ *under the phrase **Then God said.***
- *circle the word (day).*
- *underline the entire phrase referring to **time.***

As you read the text, it's helpful to have the group say the key words aloud as they mark them. This way everyone will be sure they are marking every occurrence of the word, including any synonymous words or phrases. Do this throughout the study.

DISCUSS

- What did you learn from marking the references to God and His activities in these first five verses of the Bible?

- What does God tell us about how He did what He did?

- Was anyone present besides God?

- How many days pass in verses 1–5?

- How is a day described?

OBSERVE

From Genesis 1:6 to Genesis 1:25 God tells us all that He created except for one final thing. We'll look at that next.

Leader: Read Genesis 1:26–28, 31–2:1 aloud. Once again have the group say and...
  - *mark each reference to **God**, including pronouns, with a triangle.*
  - *draw a squiggly line under the phrase **God said.***
  - *draw a box around every reference to **man**, including the pronouns:* ☐
  - *circle the word **day**.*
  - *underline the entire phrase referring to **time**.*

GENESIS 1:26–28, 31–2:1

26 Then God said, "Let Us make man in Our image, according to Our likeness; and let them rule over the fish of the sea and over the birds of the sky and over the cattle and over all the earth, and over every creeping thing that creeps on the earth."

27 God created man in His own image, in

the image of God He created him; male and female He created them.

28 God blessed them; and God said to them, "Be fruitful and multiply, and fill the earth, and subdue it; and rule over the fish of the sea and over the birds of the sky and over every living thing that moves on the earth."…

31 God saw all that He had made, and behold, it was very good. And there was evening and there was morning, the sixth day.

2:1 Thus the heavens and the earth were completed, and all their hosts.

DISCUSS

• What did you learn about God in these verses?

• What did you learn about man?

• How does this compare with what you've been taught, or what you believe, about the creation of man?

• On what day did the creation of man take place?

• If you had to summarize in one word what you've learned about God in Genesis 1:1–2:1, what word would you use, and why?

• According to all God has told us thus far in the Bible, how did He accomplish the things described in these verses?

OBSERVE

Did you notice in Genesis 1:26 the pronouns God used when speaking of the creation of man—the *Us* and *Our*? He said, "Let Us make man in Our image." Why the plural pronouns? Who is the *Us*, the *Our*? In Genesis 1:2 you saw the Spirit of God active in creation as He moved over the surface of the waters. But there is still another included in the Us.

Leader: Read John 1:1–4, 14–18 and have the group...

- *mark every reference to **the Word**, including pronouns and synonyms, with a cross:* ✝
- *mark every reference to **God** with a triangle.*
- *circle each reference to **time**, such as **beginning**, **after**, and **before**.*
- *underline each phrase referring to <u>time</u>.*

DISCUSS

- Moving verse by verse, discuss what you learned from marking the references to the Word.

JOHN 1:1–4, 14–18

1 In the beginning was the Word, and the Word was with God, and the Word was God.

2 He was in the beginning with God.

3 All things came into being through Him, and apart from Him nothing came into being that has come into being.

4 In Him was life, and the life was the Light of men....

14 And the Word became flesh, and dwelt among us, and we saw His glory, glory as of the only begotten from the Father, full of grace and truth.

15 John testified about Him and cried out, saying, "This was He of whom I said, 'He who comes after me has a higher rank than I, for He existed before me.'"

16 For of His fullness we have all received, and grace upon grace.

17 For the Law was given through Moses; grace and truth were realized through Jesus Christ.

18 No one has seen God at any time; the only begotten God who is in the bosom of the Father, He has explained Him.

• In verse 15, what did you learn from John's testimony about the Word? By the way, the text eventually makes clear that this is a reference to John the Baptist, not the apostle John who wrote this gospel.

• Read verses 17–18 again. What is the Word's name? How is He described in verse 18?

• Where was the Word in the beginning, when God created the heavens and the earth?

• How does what we've just learned fit with what we saw in Genesis?

OBSERVE

Now let's see what God the Father says about the Son.

Leader: Read Hebrews 1:8–12 slowly.
- *Have the group mark every reference to* **the Son** *with a cross. Mark all synonyms and pronouns the same way.*

DISCUSS:

- Move through this passage in Hebrews verse by verse and discuss what God tells you about the Son.

8 But of the Son He says, "Your throne, O God, is forever and ever, and the righteous scepter is the scepter of His kingdom.

9 "You have loved righteousness and hated lawlessness; therefore God, Your God, has anointed You with the oil of gladness above Your companions."

10 And, "You, Lord, in the beginning laid the foundation of the earth, and the heavens are the works of Your hands;

11 they will perish, but You remain; and they all will become old like a garment,

¹² and like a mantle You will roll them up; like a garment they will also be changed. But You are the same, and Your years will not come to an end."

• Did you see anything that would support the Son of God as being a participant in Creation? Discuss this.

COLOSSIANS 1:13–16

¹³ For He [*God*] rescued us from the domain of darkness, and transferred us to the kingdom of His beloved Son,

¹⁴ in whom we have redemption, the forgiveness of sins.

OBSERVE

There's more we need to see about the Son of God in Colossians. You'll see why you were created.

Leader: *Read Colossians 1:13–16 and have the group mark…*

- *each reference to* **God,** *including pronouns, with a triangle.*
- *every reference to God's beloved Son,* ***Jesus,*** *with a cross. Watch carefully for the pronouns.*

DISCUSS

• What did you learn from marking the references to the Son? Don't miss a thing.

• Look again at verse 16. What correlation, or similarity, do you find here with the creation account of Genesis 1?

• What, specifically, can the Son do for mankind and on what basis?

• According to Colossians 1:16, why was man created?

• If you believed that—really took it to heart—what would it mean to you personally?

15 He is the image of the invisible God, the firstborn of all creation.

16 For by Him all things were created, both in the heavens and on earth, visible and invisible, whether thrones or dominions or rulers or authorities—all things have been created through Him and for Him.

PSALM 90:1–2

¹ Lord, You have been our dwelling place in all generations.

² Before the mountains were born or You gave birth to the earth and the world, even from everlasting to everlasting, You are God.

HEBREWS 11:1–3, 6

¹ Now faith is the assurance of things hoped for, the conviction of things not seen.

² For by it the men of old gained approval.

³ By faith we understand that the worlds were prepared by the word of God, so that what is seen was not

OBSERVE

As you just read in Colossians, all things—both in the heavens and on earth, visible and invisible, whether thrones or dominions or rulers or authorities—were created through Jesus Christ.

What were they created out of? Did anything exist before creation that God used to create all He created?

Leader: Read Psalm 90:1–2 and Hebrews 11:1–3, 6 aloud. Have the group do the following:

- *Mark every reference to **God,** including pronouns, with a triangle.*
- *Draw a box around the words **born, give birth to, prepared, made.***
- *Mark the word **faith** with an **F.***

DISCUSS

- What did you learn about God from Psalm 90? This is important so don't miss a detail.

• What did you learn from marking *born, birth, prepared, made* in these two passages?

• So what was creation made from? What did God use? How did He create everything He made?

made out of things which are visible....

  6 And without faith it is impossible to please Him, for he who comes to God must believe that He is and that He is a rewarder of those who seek Him.

• Who was present at creation?

• What existed before creation?

• How do you know all this?

• Describe what the text tells you about faith and explain how that applies to your understanding of the world.

• Who are you going to believe if someone tells you anything else?

INSIGHT

If God created the world out of nothing, then He is *self-existent, self-sufficient.* To put it another way, God is *self-contained;* there is nothing He needs apart from Himself. In Exodus 3:14 God tells Moses His name is I AM—YHWH (Yahweh, or Jehovah). It comes from the word which means to exist or be. In Him is everything and anything we will ever need! And if "from everlasting to everlasting" He is God (Psalm 90:2), then He is *eternal.*

Romans 11:36 tells us "For from Him and through Him and to Him are all things. To Him be the glory forever. Amen."

Your Creator is the self-existent, self-sufficient, eternal God.

OBSERVE

As you study the Bible, you will be amazed at how often mankind is reminded that the eternal God is the Creator. This truth was emphasized by the apostles as they proclaimed the gospel, so that people might understand that God created us for His purpose (Acts 4:23–31).

Let's wrap up our study by going to the last book of the Bible, Revelation.

OBSERVE

Leader: Read Revelation 4:2, 9–11 and have the group...

- *mark with a triangle every reference to **God**, including pronouns and synonyms, such as **the One**.*
- *underline each mention of **the throne**.*

DISCUSS

- What did you learn from marking the references to God?

REVELATION 4:2, 9–11

2 Immediately I was in the Spirit; and behold, a throne was standing in heaven, and One sitting on the throne....

9 And when the living creatures give glory and honor and thanks to Him who sits on the throne, to Him who lives forever and ever,

10 the twenty-four elders will fall down before Him who sits on the throne, and will worship Him who lives forever and ever, and will cast their crowns before the throne, saying,

11 "Worthy are You, our Lord and our God, to receive glory and honor and power; for You created all things, and because of Your will they existed, and were created."

• According to verse 11, why do you exist?

• Do you believe God is the Creator? Why or why not?

• Do you think God is really worthy to receive glory and honor and power? Why?

OBSERVE

Let's look at one last passage that ties in with what you just saw in Revelation 4. It is a description of what happens when Jesus, the Lamb of God, appears before the throne of God and all the heavenly host surrounding the throne. Verse 9 describes the Lamb as "standing, as if slain," so this occurs after Jesus' death, burial, resurrection, and ascension into heaven.

Leader: Read Revelation 5:11–13 and have the group mark...

- *every reference to* **the Lamb** *with a cross.*
- *the reference to* **God,** *described here as* **Him who sits on the throne,** *with a triangle.*

DISCUSS

- What did you learn from marking the references to the Lamb?

REVELATION 5:11–13

11 Then I looked, and I heard the voice of many angels around the throne and the living creatures and the elders; and the number of them was myriads of myriads, and thousands of thousands,

12 saying with a loud voice, "Worthy is the Lamb that was slain to receive power and riches and wisdom

and might and honor and glory and blessing."

13 And every created thing which is in heaven and on the earth and under the earth and on the sea, and all things in them, I heard saying, "To Him who sits on the throne, and to the Lamb, be blessing and honor and glory and dominion forever and ever."

• What did you learn from marking the reference to God?

• If you truly believe God and Jesus Christ, the Lamb, are to have dominion (supreme authority to rule) forever and ever, how will that affect your life?

• How would that look, practically speaking, in your day-to-day life?

... in the way you spend your time, your money?

... in the way you dress, talk, behave, treat others, do your job?

... in what you watch, read, do?

WRAP IT UP

As you read though the Word of God, you will find God Himself reminding His people time and time again that He is the Creator of the heavens and the earth. Because of that, as Jeremiah says, "Nothing is too difficult" for Him (32:17, 27). Our self-existent, self-sufficient Creator needs nothing from us—and since we were created for His purposes, our role is to submit to Him, giving Him glory and honor in every aspect of our lives.

When Job endured unmerited suffering, he received all sorts of confusing explanations from his friends. Job himself questioned why a righteous, God-fearing man like him should be subject to such misery. Finally the Lord answered Job out of the whirlwind,

Who is this that darkens counsel
By words without knowledge?
Now gird up your loins like a man,
And I will ask you, and you instruct Me!
Where were you when I laid the foundation of the earth?
Tell Me, if you have understanding. (Job 38:2–4)

For two chapters God bombarded Job with questions while giving breath-taking explanations of His creation. Finally, overwhelmed by truth, Job responded,

Behold, I am insignificant; what can I reply to You?
I lay my hand on my mouth.

Once I have spoken, and I will not answer;
Even twice, and I will add nothing more. (Job 40:4–5)

Job became putty in the hands of the Divine Potter, willing to be shaped in any way God desired.

Such surrender will mark our attitude as well, once we truly know our God.

Why don't you, as a group, take time to worship your Creator, the everlasting God. To worship is to look at someone's worth, to bow before Him, to rehearse who He is, tell Him He is Worthy, and submit all to Him.

And really, what other response can we have, knowing that we exist because of Him…and for Him?

As we saw in our first lesson, Genesis, the book of beginnings, tells us that God is the Creator of the heavens and the earth. We learned that all three Persons of the Godhead (often referred to as the Trinity) were present at Creation, including God the Son. All that exists, we are told, exists because of Him and through Him. He is the first-born of all Creation—the One who was before all things. His name is Jesus.

We also saw, in Revelation, that one day all of creation will worship the God who created all things. We read that the Father and the Son are worthy not only to receive "blessing and honor and glory" but also "dominion forever and ever" (Revelation 5:13).

"Dominion forever and ever" is another way of saying that God rules in sovereignty over all the universe. What does that mean? What does that look like? How is it possible? This is what we will explore this week as we get to know our God. Surely such knowledge will bring stability, strength, and the ability to act, to live as our Creator intends.

OBSERVE

The book of Psalms is the Bible's book of prayer. This compilation of praise, prayer, songs, and the outpouring of man's soul gives us great insights into who God is. In this discourse between man and God you discover a wealth of insight into His attributes, His character, and His relationship to His creation. Therefore this is where we will begin.

PSALM 103:19–22

19 The LORD has established His throne in the heavens, and His sovereignty rules over all.

20 Bless the LORD, you His angels, mighty in strength, who perform His word, obeying the voice of His word!

21 Bless the LORD, all you His hosts, you who serve Him, doing His will.

22 Bless the LORD, all you works of His, in all places of His dominion; bless the LORD, O my soul!

Leader: Read Psalm 103:19–22 aloud and have the group …

- *mark every reference to **the Lord,** including pronouns, with a triangle.*
- *draw a squiggly line under every occurrence of **bless.***

Remind the group to say each word or phrase aloud as they mark it.

DISCUSS

- Verse by verse, discuss what you learned about the Lord.

- What did you learn about God's sovereignty in verse 19? (This would be a good verse to memorize.)

- Who is to bless the Lord ?

• What did you learn about those who bless Him?

INSIGHT

The root of the Hebrew word *barak* means "to kneel, to bless." In respect to blessing God, it would imply attributing to God the praise that is due Him, recognizing who God is and what He has done, and thanking Him.

• How do the actions of the angels and God's hosts demonstrate God's rule, His dominion—or to use another word, His sovereignty?

Isaiah 40:12, 21–26

12 Who has measured the waters in the hollow of His hand, and marked off the heavens by the span, and calculated the dust of the earth by the measure, and weighed the mountains in a balance and the hills in a pair of scales?...

21 Do you not know? Have you not heard? Has it not been declared to you from the beginning? Have you not understood from the foundations of the earth?

22 It is He who sits above the circle of the earth, and its inhabitants are like grasshoppers, who stretches out the heavens like a curtain

OBSERVE

Because the Bible is the Word of God, scripture will never contradict scripture; rather scripture becomes the best interpreter of scripture. This means that, rather than looking at single verses in isolation, we need to consider the whole of the Bible. God wants to be understood; therefore, He reveals truth in numerous ways, tucking these insights many times throughout His book. In the light of this, let's explore some other verses that demonstrate the sovereignty of God—His dominion over all.

Leader: Read Isaiah 40:12 without marking anything. Then read verses 21–26 and have the group...

- *mark every reference to **the Creator**, including pronouns and synonyms such as **Holy One** and **One** with a triangle.*
- *circle every reference to **time**.*

DISCUSS

- In order to better put you into the context of Isaiah 40:21–26, we picked up verse 12. What is the answer to the question posed in verse 12?

- Carefully discuss what you learned from marking the references to God. As you do, notice the various things that are stated as being under God's dominion, or sovereignty.

- According to these verses, is anyone or anything equal to or above God?

- How do these verses, including verse 12, support God as the Creator?

and spreads them out like a tent to dwell in.

23 He it is who reduces rulers to nothing, who makes the judges of the earth meaningless.

24 Scarcely have they been planted, scarcely have they been sown, scarcely has their stock taken root in the earth, but He merely blows on them, and they wither, and the storm carries them away like stubble.

25 "To whom then will you liken Me that I would be his equal?" says the Holy One.

26 Lift up your eyes on high and see who has created these stars, the One who leads

forth their host by number, He calls them all by name; because of the greatness of His might and the strength of His power, not one of them is missing.

• Pause now and think about what you have learned today just from these two segments of Scripture. Does such knowledge have any practical value? Explain your answer.

DANIEL 4:30–37

30 The king reflected and said, "Is this not Babylon the great, which I myself have built as a royal residence by the might of my power and for the glory of my majesty?"

31 While the word was in the king's mouth, a voice came from heaven, saying, "King Nebuchadnezzar, to you it is declared: sovereignty has been removed from you,

OBSERVE

In the Old Testament one of the most memorable demonstrations of God's sovereignty is described in Daniel 4. The event occurs during the reign of Nebuchadnezzar, the king of Babylon—the most powerful ruler of the Middle East.

The opening verses of Daniel 4 describe Nebuchadnezzar having a disturbing dream, a dream which is interpreted by Daniel, an Israelite taken captive during Babylon's first siege of Jerusalem. Daniel explains that the dream is a warning from God of what will happen to the king if he does not "break away now from your sins by doing righteousness and from your iniquities by showing mercy to the poor, in case there may be a prolonging of your prosperity" (Daniel 4:27).

We will pick up the story twelve months later, to see how Nebuchadnezzar responded to the warning.

Leader: Read Daniel 4:30–37 aloud. Have the group...

- *mark each reference to **Nebuchadnezzar**, the king, with an **X**. Watch carefully for the pronouns.*
- *draw a triangle over every reference to **the Most High**, including pronouns and synonyms.*

DISCUSS

- What did God tell Nebuchadnezzar would happen to him?

- According to verse 32, what did Nebuchadnezzar need to recognize?

32 and you will be driven away from mankind, and your dwelling place will be with the beasts of the field. You will be given grass to eat like cattle, and seven periods of time will pass over you until you recognize that the Most High is ruler over the realm of mankind and bestows it on whomever He wishes."

33 Immediately the word concerning Nebuchadnezzar was fulfilled; and he was driven away from mankind and began eating grass like cattle, and his body was drenched with the dew of heaven until his hair had grown like eagles' feathers and his nails like birds' claws.

34 "But at the end of that period, I, Nebuchadnezzar, raised my eyes toward heaven and my reason returned to me, and I blessed the Most High and praised and honored Him who lives forever; for His dominion is an everlasting dominion, and His kingdom endures from generation to generation.

35 "All the inhabitants of the earth are accounted as nothing, but He does according to His will in the host of heaven and among the inhabitants of earth; and no one can ward off His hand or

• Did the king ever do this? How did he refer to God? By what name does the king call God?

• What happened to bring Nebuchadnezzar into submission?

• What does this tell you about God and His power?

• What did Nebuchadnezzar learn and confess about God in verses 34–35? Don't miss a detail.

- Where is God's will done, according to verse 35? This is important to note, because we know from the Word of God that good and bad angelic beings, including Satan, have access to heaven.

- What was Nebuchadnezzar's response to God in verse 37? What reason did he give for his actions?

- How can understanding God as the Most High who rules over all affect your life when things seem difficult, unfair, hopeless, or more than you can bear?

- What about when you consider rebelling against God, or are tempted to take pride in your achievements?

say to Him, 'What have You done?'

36 "At that time my reason returned to me. And my majesty and splendor were restored to me for the glory of my kingdom, and my counselors and my nobles began seeking me out; so I was reestablished in my sovereignty, and surpassing greatness was added to me.

37 "Now I, Nebuchadnezzar, praise, exalt and honor the King of heaven, for all His works are true and His ways just, and He is able to humble those who walk in pride."

DEUTERONOMY 32:39

See now that I, I am He, and there is no god besides Me; it is I who put to death and give life. I have wounded and it is I who heal, and there is no one who can deliver from My hand.

1 SAMUEL 2:6–10

6 The LORD kills and makes alive; He brings down to Sheol and raises up.

7 The LORD makes poor and rich; He brings low, He also exalts.

8 He raises the poor from the dust, He lifts the needy from the ash heap to make them sit with nobles, and in-herit a seat of honor;

OBSERVE:

Let's look at several verses that highlight various truths about the all-encompassing sovereignty of the Most High God.

Leader: Read the texts one by one, beginning with Deuteronomy 32:39 and finishing with 1 Corinthians 10:13. Have the group…
- *mark the references to **God,** including pronouns and synonyms, with a triangle.*
- *mark the references to **Jesus,** including pronouns, with a cross.*
- *underline any references to **people,** such as **no one, nobles, poor, rich,** etc.*

After you read each passage, stop and discuss what you observed.

INSIGHT

In 1 Samuel 2:6–10, *Sheol* is a ref-erence to the grave, to death—not to one's final destination or to hell. Don't miss what verse 6 tells you.

DISCUSS

• What did you learn from marking the references to God, Jesus, and the people?

• What is God sovereign over in each passage?

for the pillars of the earth are the LORD's, and He set the world on them.

9 He keeps the feet of His godly ones, but the wicked ones are silenced in darkness; for not by might shall a man prevail.

10 Those who contend with the LORD will be shattered; against them He will thunder in the heavens, the LORD will judge the ends of the earth.

ISAIAH 45:5–7

5 I am the LORD, and there is no other; besides Me there is no God. I will gird you, though you have not known Me;

6 that men may know from the rising to the setting of the sun that there is no one besides Me. I am the LORD, and there is no other,

7 the One forming light and creating darkness, causing well-being and creating calamity; I am the LORD who does all these.

JOHN 19:10–11

Jesus has been arrested by the Sanhedrin and taken to Pilate, the Roman governor.

10 So Pilate said to Him, "You do not speak to me? Do You not know that I have authority to release You, and I have authority to crucify You?"

INSIGHT

This passage from Isaiah is a prophecy about Cyrus, king of Persia, who will not be on the scene of history for about another 150 years. He is the *you* of verse 5.

11 Jesus answered, "You would have no authority over Me, unless it had been given you from above; for this reason he who delivered Me to you has the greater sin."

• Discuss how God can guarantee what He says in 1 Corinthians 10:13.

1 CORINTHIANS 10:13

No temptation has overtaken you but such as is common to man; and God is faithful, who will not allow you to be tempted beyond what you are able, but with the temptation will provide the way of escape also, so that you will be able to endure it.

PSALM 33:6–15

6 By the word of the LORD the heavens were made, and by the breath of His mouth all their host.

7 He gathers the waters of the sea together as a heap; He lays up the deeps in storehouses.

8 Let all the earth fear the LORD; let all the inhabitants of the world stand in awe of Him.

9 For He spoke, and it was done; He commanded, and it stood fast.

10 The LORD nullifies the counsel of the nations; He frustrates the plans of the peoples.

OBSERVE

Since we opened this week's study in Psalms, let's return there before we wrap it up.

Leader: Read Psalm 33:6–15 aloud. Have the group...

- *mark every reference to **the Lord**, including pronouns, with a triangle.*
- *underline references to **people**, such as **inhabitants**, **nations**.*

DISCUSS

- What did you learn from marking the references to the Lord?

- What did you learn from marking the references to the people?

- Discuss how these verses apply to people today.

- How can what you learned today help you pray for others?

- Close your time today by blessing the Lord, praising Him for who He is, for what you have learned, and for giving you the opportunity to do this study.

- Then, ask the Lord, in His sovereignty, to lead you to someone who needs to know what you have learned.

11 The counsel of the LORD stands forever, the plans of His heart from generation to generation.

12 Blessed is the nation whose God is the LORD, the people whom He has chosen for His own inheritance.

13 The LORD looks from heaven; He sees all the sons of men;

14 From His dwelling place He looks out on all the inhabitants of the earth,

15 He who fashions the hearts of them all, He who understands all their works.

WRAP IT UP

If you were to read the Bible from cover to cover and simply put a triangle in the margin of the page at each place you learn something about God, it would transform your life—if you took those truths to heart.

In the process you would gain insight upon insight into the sovereignty of God. And with each insight your faith would be strengthened, as you realize the Bible affirms over and over again that God is the supreme ruler of all the universe, in absolute control. Nothing—absolutely nothing—can happen without His permission. Whether or not we understand it, God's eternal purpose will be accomplished. He tells us in Isaiah 46:11, "Truly I have spoken; truly I will bring it to pass. I have planned it, surely I will do it." Nothing that He created can stop Him. He is greater than all and sovereign over creation.

What inexplicable peace, confidence, and rest it can bring to your life to understand the character of this One who is supremely sovereign.

We will continue to explore what God says about Himself over the next four weeks. If you believe and act on what you learn, you'll discover how beloved you are to God—and with that knowledge will come strength and a sense of peace you may never have known before.

So often we judge God—His person, His ability, His activity or lack of action—based on how we would handle things if we were running the world. When our conversations touch on the reality of a personal God to whom we might be accountable, we often hear people say things like, "Surely if there is a God, He would _____" (fill in the blank). Or, "If God is God, how can He allow these things to happen?"

As you explored God's Word in the past two lessons, you saw that God repeatedly states that He is the Creator—"all things came into being through Him" (John 1:3). You also saw that the Creator is sovereign, reigning supreme over all. None can rightfully question what He's doing (Daniel 4:34–35).

Yet people do question God, don't they?

Could that be because they do not really know what makes God, God? What makes the Most High different from, and in all ways above, man? Beyond our limited comprehension?

Could there be a purpose to all that our sovereign God does, even if we do not know it? Is a divine plan at work in this world? In our lives? Is it possible that God really does know what He's doing?

Before we bring God before the tribunal of our limited understanding and bring down the gavel, shouting "Guilty," let's see what else God tells us about Himself. What peace and confidence and courage it will bring!

ISAIAH 46:8–10

8 Remember this, and be assured; recall it to mind, you transgressors.

9 Remember the former things long past, for I am God, and there is no other; I am God, and there is no one like Me,

10 declaring the end from the beginning, and from ancient times things which have not been done, saying, "My purpose will be established, and I will accomplish all My good pleasure."

OBSERVE

Leader: *Read Isaiah 46:8–10 aloud. Have the group say and mark...*

- *each occurrence of the words* **remember** *or* **recall it to mind** *with a check mark, like this:* ✓
- *all references to* **God,** *including pronouns, with a triangle:* △

DISCUSS

- What did you learn from marking the references to God in these verses?

- What are the implications of these truths? If you believed this, how would it affect the way you live?

- How do the truths in these verses relate to what you've learned about God as Creator and Sovereign?

- What does God expect the reader to do with this information? (Hint: Look at the other words you marked.)

OBSERVE

How well does this God of purpose know and understand you as an individual? Let's take a look at Psalm 139 and see what else we can learn about Him.

Leader: Read Psalm 139:1–6 aloud. Have the group say and...

- *mark all references to **Lord,** including pronouns, with a triangle.*
- *circle each pronoun referring to **the psalmist**—each **me, I,** and **my.***
- *underline **known, know,** and **knowledge.***

DISCUSS

- What did you learn about God from these verses? What are the qualities, or abilities, that He possesses as God, as described in this passage?

- Look for the words *know, known,* and *knowledge.* What does the context of each in this passage tell you about God?

PSALM 139:1–6

¹ O LORD, You have searched me and known me.

² You know when I sit down and when I rise up; You understand my thought from afar.

³ You scrutinize my path and my lying down, and are intimately acquainted with all my ways.

⁴ Even before there is a word on my tongue, behold, O LORD, You know it all.

⁵ You have enclosed me behind and before, and laid Your hand upon me.

6 Such knowledge is too wonderful for me; it is too high, I cannot attain to it.

• Did you know these things about God? How does this knowledge make you feel?

INSIGHT

In an effort to help people know God—to understand the attributes that make Him God—theologians have used various words to describe His attributes; among them are the terms *omniscience, omnipotence,* and *omnipresence.*

Omni (meaning "all") is combined with three different words. Combined with *science* (knowledge), *omniscience* means God knows everything. There is nothing God does not know, because that would violate His very nature as God.

Leader: *Have the group review the meanings of* omniscience, omnipotence, *and* omnipresence *as described in the Insight box. Then read Psalm 139:1–6 aloud again and have the group call out any of these attributes mentioned in those verses.*

Omnipotence means God is all powerful; He is potent. No one and nothing is more powerful than He. His power is inherent, part of His being as God.

Omnipresence means there is no place where God is not present. Absolutely nothing is beyond God's reach. To be clear, this is *not* saying that He is in everything; that is "pantheism," a mistaken belief that God is in everything—such as trees, flowers, etc.—which is contrary to the Word of God in its totality and context.

PSALM 139:7–12

7 Where can I go from Your Spirit? Or where can I flee from Your presence?

8 If I ascend to heaven, You are there; if I make my bed in Sheol, behold, You are there.

9 If I take the wings of the dawn, if I dwell in the remotest part of the sea,

10 even there Your hand will lead me, and Your right hand will lay hold of me.

11 If I say, "Surely the darkness will overwhelm me, and the light around me will be night,"

12 even the darkness is not dark to You, and the night is as bright as the day. Darkness and light are alike to You.

OBSERVE

Leader: Read Psalm 139:7–12 aloud and have the group...
- *mark every reference to **God**, including pronouns, with a triangle.*
- *circle each pronoun—each **I, my,** and **me.***

DISCUSS

• Did you see any evidence of or reference to the "omnis" of God in these verses? If so, which ones?

• You marked *I, my,* and *me.* Do you think this pertains to you? Explain your answer.

• If so, how would it affect you, as an individual, to be known by God in all these ways?

OBSERVE

Leader: Read Psalm 139:13–18, 23–24 and have the group...

- *mark every reference to **God**, including pronouns, with a triangle.*
- *circle each **I, my,** and **me.***

DISCUSS

- Once again discuss anything you noticed in these verses that touches on truths you have learned about God thus far in this study.

PSALM 139:13–18, 23–24

13 For You formed my inward parts; You wove me in my mother's womb.

14 I will give thanks to You, for I am fearfully and wonderfully made; wonderful are Your works, and my soul knows it very well.

15 My frame was not hidden from You, when I was made in secret, and skillfully wrought in the depths of the earth;

16 Your eyes have seen my unformed substance; and in Your book were all written the days that were ordained for me, when as yet there was not one of them.

17 How precious also are Your thoughts to

me, O God! How vast is the sum of them!

18 If I should count them, they would outnumber the sand. When I awake, I am still with You....

23 Search me, O God, and know my heart; try me and know my anxious thoughts;

24 and see if there be any hurtful way in me, and lead me in the everlasting way.

MATTHEW 10:29–31

29 Are not two sparrows sold for a cent? And yet not one of them will fall to the ground apart from your Father.

30 But the very hairs of your head are all numbered.

• Did you learn anything about yourself in these verses that really touches your heart? A truth that helps you deal with some issues you might have with God or with your personal life? If so, please share that with the group.

OBSERVE

Now let's look beyond Psalm 139 to other scriptures that help us glimpse the scope of God's knowledge, His omniscience.

Leader: *Read Matthew 10:29–31; Psalm 44:20–21; Jeremiah 12:3; Luke 16:14–15; Hebrews 4:13. Have the group...*

- *draw a triangle over each reference to* **God the Father.**
- *mark each reference to* **Jesus** *with a cross.*
- *mark every reference to* **the heart,** *with a heart like this:*

DISCUSS

- Discuss what you learned from each passage in respect to God's omniscience and the heart of man.

31 So do not fear; you are more valuable than many sparrows.

PSALM 44:20–21

20 If we had forgotten the name of our God or extended our hands to a strange god,

21 would not God find this out? For He knows the secrets of the heart.

JEREMIAH 12:3

But You know me, O LORD; You see me; and You examine my heart's attitude toward You.

LUKE 16:14–15

14 Now the Pharisees, who were lovers of money, were listening to all these things and were scoffing at Him [*Jesus*].

15 And He said to them, "You are those who justify

yourselves in the sight of men, but God knows your hearts; for that which is highly esteemed among men is detestable in the sight of God."

HEBREWS 4:13

And there is no creature hidden from His sight, but all things are open and laid bare to the eyes of Him with whom we have to do.

PROVERBS 15:3

The eyes of the LORD are in every place, watching the evil and the good.

2 CHRONICLES 16:7-9

7 At that time Hanani the seer came to Asa king of Judah and said to him, "Because you have relied on the king of

OBSERVE

Leader: *Read Proverbs 15:3 and 2 Chronicles 16:7–9. Have the group...*

- *draw a triangle over each reference to* **the Lord,** *including pronouns.*
- *draw a box around each occurrence of the word* **relied.**
- *mark* **heart** *with a heart.*

DISCUSS

- What did you learn from marking the references to the Lord?

- Did you see any other attribute of God noted in these verses, besides His omniscience? Discuss the insights of the group.

- What did you learn from marking *relied*?

- What did you learn from marking *heart*?

- What does Asa's reliance on the king of Aram suggest about his heart? What can you personally learn from this?

- Does the truth of 2 Chronicles 16:9a go beyond Asa? Would it apply to you? Give the reason for your answer.

- How could knowing this impact a person's life?

Aram and have not relied on the LORD your God, therefore the army of the king of Aram has escaped out of your hand.

8 "Were not the Ethiopians and the Lubim an immense army with very many chariots and horsemen? Yet because you relied on the LORD, He delivered them into your hand.

9 "For the eyes of the LORD move to and fro throughout the earth that He may strongly support those whose heart is completely His. You have acted foolishly in this. Indeed, from now on you will surely have wars."

2 CHRONICLES 20:5–12

⁵ Then Jehoshaphat stood in the assembly of Judah and Jerusalem, in the house of the LORD before the new court,

⁶ and he said, "O LORD, the God of our fathers, are You not God in the heavens? And are You not ruler over all the kingdoms of the nations? Power and might are in Your hand so that no one can stand against You.

⁷ "Did You not, O our God, drive out the inhabitants of this land before Your people Israel and give it to the descendants of Abraham Your friend forever?

⁸ "They have lived in it, and have built

OBSERVE

Let's look now at several verses that demonstrate God's omnipotence. The first passage we'll examine, 2 Chronicles 20:5–12, records a portion of King Jehoshaphat's prayer to the Lord when this ruler of Judah heard that a great multitude was coming against him in war.

Leader: Read 2 Chronicles 20:5–12.

- *Have the group say aloud and mark every reference to **God**, including pronouns and synonyms, with a triangle.*

DISCUSS

- What did Jehoshaphat remember about the Lord's past actions?

• How did he use this knowledge?

• What lessons do you find in this for our lives today?

You a sanctuary there for Your name, saying,

9 'Should evil come upon us, the sword, or judgment, or pestilence, or famine, we will stand before this house and before You (for Your name is in this house) and cry to You in our distress, and You will hear and deliver us.'

10 "Now behold, the sons of Ammon and Moab and Mount Seir, whom You did not let Israel invade when they came out of the land of Egypt (they turned aside from them and did not destroy them),

11 see how they are rewarding us by coming to drive us out

from Your possession which You have given us as an inheritance.

12 "O our God, will You not judge them? For we are powerless before this great multitude who are coming against us; nor do we know what to do, but our eyes are on You."

DANIEL 2:19–23, 27–28

19 Then the mystery was revealed to Daniel in a night vision. Then Daniel blessed the God of heaven;

20 Daniel said, "Let the name of God be blessed forever and ever, for wisdom and power belong to Him.

21 "It is He who changes the times and

By the way, 2 Chronicles chapter 20 goes on to describe how God marvelously delivered the king and his people. It's worth reading when you have the time. There is so much to learn and apply.

OBSERVE

Let's close with some powerful words of praise from the prophet Daniel. He spoke these words after God spared his life and his friends by giving Daniel insight to interpret a dream of Nebuchadnezzar, king of Babylon.

Leader: *Read Daniel 2:19–23, 27–28.*
  • *Have the group say aloud and mark every reference to **God,** including pronouns, with a triangle.*

DISCUSS

• What did you learn about God from this passage? What specific attributes are described in these verses?

• What did you see Daniel doing in these verses? What did you notice about how he speaks to and about God?

• What have you learned about the practicality of knowing God? How can these truths help you personally with whatever is happening in your life today?

the epochs; He removes kings and establishes kings; He gives wisdom to wise men and knowledge to men of understanding.

22 "It is He who reveals the profound and hidden things; He knows what is in the darkness, and the light dwells with Him.

23 "To You, O God of my fathers, I give thanks and praise, for You have given me wisdom and power; even now You have made known to me what we requested of You, for You have made known to us the king's matter."...

27 Daniel answered before the king and

said, "As for the mystery about which the king has inquired, neither wise men, conjurers, magicians nor diviners are able to declare it to the king.

28 "However, there is a God in heaven who reveals mysteries, and He has made known to King Nebuchadnezzar what will take place in the latter days."

• Why don't you spend some time as a group worshiping God, as Daniel did, for specific truths He has taught you in this lesson.

WRAP IT UP

Doesn't it bring great peace and confidence to know that God knows everything, that there is no hiding from Him? That He is all powerful?

There is nothing God cannot do, for He is the God of all flesh. Nothing is impossible for Him as we saw earlier. Omnipotent, omniscient, omnipresent—these attributes of God mean you are never alone and never without help if you are a child of God.

We may not understand all that God allows to happen. The reason for our circumstances or for events in the world may be a mystery to us, but not to Almighty God. Knowing who God is, what He is capable of, and that He has encompassed us with His presence from conception to and through physical death ought to bring us such comfort and confidence. How clear it is that our times are in His hands! And if they are in His hands we need not fear man.

Listen to what God says in Isaiah 43:1–3:

> *But now, thus says the LORD, your Creator, O Jacob,*
> *And He who formed you, O Israel,*
> *"Do not fear, for I have redeemed you;*
> *I have called you by name; you are Mine!*
> *When you pass through the waters, I will be with you;*
> *And through the rivers, they will not overflow you.*
> *When you walk through the fire, you will not be scorched,*
> *Nor will the flame burn you.*
> *For I am the LORD your God,*
> *The Holy One of Israel, your Savior."*

So far in this study we have seen that the everlasting God, the Creator of all, is the Sovereign Ruler of heaven and earth. Omniscient—He knows all. Omnipotent—He is all powerful. Omnipresent—there is no hiding from Him.

But how does He wield His unparalleled power?

Many despots have sat upon thrones, reigning recklessly, capriciously, even mercilessly as they brandished the power of life and death over their subjects. Some started well, made grand promises, but then consumed by their own glory and power, crushed their own people under the heel of their tyranny.

Would God ever do that? What kind of a ruler is He? Can He be trusted—or should we run and hide in terror?

These are valid questions. If we want valid answers rather than the speculations of human beings, then we must look in the Bible to see what kind of ruler God has proven Himself to be.

OBSERVE

Leader: *Read Psalm 89:14 aloud. Have the group mark…*

- *every reference to* **God**—*the* **Your** *and* **You**—*with a triangle.*
- *the word* **truth** *with a big* **T.**

PSALM 89:14

Righteousness and justice are the foundation of Your throne; lovingkindness and truth go before You.

DISCUSS

• What did you learn about God from this verse?

• What is the basis, the foundation, from which God rules?

• What two things "go before God"? In other words, what comes as a result of His rule?

• If someone were to ask you what God is like as a person, and all you had was this one verse, how would you describe Him?

• Now think about what you have just seen. What assurance does such knowledge give you and how does it apply, practically, to your life?

• Can God be trusted? How do you know?

OBSERVE

Now let's read Psalm 89:14 in its context to get a fuller picture of the truths we've just seen.

Leader: Read Psalm 89:5–14 aloud.

- *Once again, have the group mark every reference to **the Lord**, including pronouns, with a triangle.*

DISCUSS

- What did you learn about God from these verses?

- What words are used to describe God?

- We've covered this before, but to be sure you don't miss it, what is the basis of God's authority? (Look again at verse 11 if you need a reminder.)

PSALM 89:5–14

5 The heavens will praise Your wonders, O LORD; Your faithfulness also in the assembly of the holy ones.

6 For who in the skies is comparable to the LORD? Who among the sons of the mighty is like the LORD,

7 a God greatly feared in the council of the holy ones, and awesome above all those who are around Him?

8 O LORD God of hosts, who is like You, O mighty LORD? Your faithfulness also surrounds You.

9 You rule the swelling of the sea; when its waves rise, You still them.

10 You Yourself crushed Rahab [*sea monster*] like one who is slain; You scattered Your enemies with Your mighty arm.

11 The heavens are Yours, the earth also is Yours; the world and all it contains, You have founded them.

12 The north and the south, You have created them; Tabor and Hermon [*two mountains in the land of Israel*] shout for joy at Your name.

13 You have a strong arm; Your hand is mighty, Your right hand is exalted.

INSIGHT

The three attributes of God that we want to focus on at this point are *righteousness, justice,* and *truth.* Because words convey thoughts and give information, it is important to understand what they mean.

Righteousness refers to that which is right, not according to man but according to what God says is right. God Himself determines what is right and what is wrong. Righteousness is not relative. It is an unchanging standard that is in accord with the Word of truth, the Word of God.

Justice is intimately connected to righteousness; you cannot separate them. Justice refers to equity, fairness, that which is right.

The foundation of God's throne is righteousness and justice because God is righteous and just. God can never act apart from what He is. For that reason lovingkindness and truth go before God.

Lovingkindness, or *hesed* in the Hebrew, speaks of God's grace and favor, which we will examine in greater depth in next week's lesson.

Truth signifies God's absolutely veracity. In 2 Samuel 7:28, David declares, "You are God, and Your words are truth." If God were not truth, He could not be righteous or just.

¹⁴ Righteousness and justice are the foundation of Your throne; lovingkindness and truth go before You.

OBSERVE

Near the end of Moses' life, when he was 120 years old, Moses instructed that every seven years the book of the law would be read in its entirety to the people of Israel— "the men and the women and children and the alien who is in your town, so that they may hear and learn and fear the LORD your God, and be careful to observe all the words of this law" (Deuteronomy 31:12). The teaching of the people included a song that would serve as a witness to God. Let's look at how God is described in the beginning of the song.

DEUTERONOMY 32:3–4

3 For I proclaim the name of the LORD; ascribe greatness to our God!

4 The Rock! His work is perfect, for all His ways are just; a God of faithfulness and without injustice, righteous and upright is He.

Leader: Read Deuteronomy 32:3–4 aloud.

• *Have the group draw a triangle over every reference to* **God,** *including synonyms and pronouns.*

DISCUSS

• What did you learn from Moses about God?

• According to these two verses, what moral attributes of God were to be remembered in this song?

• How does this compare with what you just saw in Psalm 89:14?

PSALM 111:7

The works of His hands are truth and justice; all His precepts are sure.

OBSERVE

We've seen that justice and righteousness are the foundation of God's throne, and truth goes before God. Let's look next at some verses that describe God's justice.

Leader: *Read aloud Psalm 111:7; Deuteronomy 10:17–18; Isaiah 30:18; Romans 9:14; Genesis 18:25; and Micah 6:8. Have the group do the following:*

- *Draw a triangle over the references to* **God.**
- *Mark the words* **justice** *and* **justly,** *with a* **J.**
- *Mark* **injustice** *the same way, but put a slash through it:* **J**
- *Mark a big* **T** *over the word* **truth.**

DISCUSS

- What did you learn from marking *justice* and *justly?*

DEUTERONOMY 10:17–18

17 For the LORD your God is the God of gods and the Lord of lords, the great, the mighty, and the awesome God who does not show partiality nor take a bribe.

18 He executes justice for the orphan and the widow, and shows His love for the alien by giving him food and clothing.

ISAIAH 30:18

Therefore the LORD longs to be gracious to you, and therefore He waits on high to have compassion on you. For the LORD is a God of justice; how blessed are all those who long for Him.

ROMANS 9:14

What shall we say then? There is no injustice with God, is there? May it never be!

GENESIS 18:25

Far be it from You to do such a thing, to slay the righteous with the wicked, so that the righteous and the wicked are treated alike. Far be it from You! Shall not the Judge of all the earth deal justly?

MICAH 6:8

He has told you, O man, what is good; and what does the LORD require of you but to do justice, to love kindness, and to walk humbly with your God?

• What are the ways we see God's justice revealed in these verses?

• Knowing this about God, what do you think God would expect from His children when it comes to justice?

• How do these verses impact your trust in God?

OBSERVE

Let's look at some verses that specifically mention the righteousness of God and answer the question, "If God allows us to go through difficulties, does that make Him unrighteous?"

Leader: Read Psalm 71:18–20; 145:17–20; and 119:142 slowly and carefully. Have the group…

- *draw a triangle over the references to **God**, including synonyms and pronouns.*
- *mark each occurrence of the words **righteousness** and **righteous** with an **R**.*
- *mark the word **truth** with a **T**.*
- *draw a squiggly line like this ⌣⌣⌣ under all references to **difficulties, destruction**.*

DISCUSS

- What did you learn from marking the references to God?

PSALM 71:18–20

18 And even when I am old and gray, O God, do not forsake me, until I declare Your strength to this generation, Your power to all who are to come.

19 For Your righteousness, O God, reaches to the heavens, You who have done great things; O God, who is like You?

20 You who have shown me many troubles and distresses will revive me again, and will bring me up again from the depths of the earth.

PSALM 145:17–20

17 The LORD is righteous in all His ways and kind in all His deeds.

18 The LORD is near to all who call upon Him, to all who call upon Him in truth.

19 He will fulfill the desire of those who fear Him; He will also hear their cry and will save them.

20 The LORD keeps all who love Him, but all the wicked He will destroy.

PSALM 119:142

Your righteousness is an everlasting righteousness, and Your law is truth.

• Let's focus on His righteousness. What did you learn from marking the words *righteous* and *righteousness*?

• How do you see God's righteousness manifested in Psalm 145:19–20 in respect to those who fear God—those who honor, respect Him—and the wicked, who do not?

• Do difficulties, death, or destruction alter or nullify the righteousness of God? Explain your answer.

• How long will God be righteous? Discuss the benefits of knowing this.

OBSERVE

Let's look at two passages in the book of Revelation that show another aspect of the righteousness of the throne of God. These events, which speak of God's judgment, are yet to occur.

Leader: Read Revelation 15:1–4 and 16:4–7 aloud and have the group do the following:

- *Draw a triangle over the references to **the Lord God**, including synonyms and pronouns.*
- *Mark an **R** over the word **righteous**.*
- *Mark a **T** over the words **truth** and **true**.*
- *Mark **plagues, wrath,** or any reference to **the judgment of God** with a bolt of lightning like this:* ⚡

DISCUSS

- What did you learn about the Lord God from these verses?

REVELATION 15:1–4

1 Then I saw another sign in heaven, great and marvelous, seven angels who had seven plagues, which are the last, because in them the wrath of God is finished.

2 And I saw something like a sea of glass mixed with fire, and those who had been victorious over the beast and his image and the number of his name, standing on the sea of glass, holding harps of God.

3 And they sang the song of Moses, the bond-servant of God, and the song of the Lamb, saying, "Great and marvelous are Your

works, O Lord God, the Almighty; righteous and true are Your ways, King of the nations!

4 "Who will not fear, O Lord, and glorify Your name? For You alone are holy; for all the nations will come and worship before You, for Your righteous acts have been revealed."

REVELATION 16:4–7

4 Then the third angel poured out his bowl into the rivers and the springs of waters; and they became blood.

5 And I heard the angel of the waters saying, "Righteous are You, who are and who were, O Holy One,

• How are the righteousness and justice of God manifested in these verses?

• Do you see any connection between God's righteousness and His judgment?

• Do you think people expect this from God? Why or why not?

• According to the Word of God, is God's judgment right or wrong?

because You judged these things;

6 for they poured out the blood of saints and prophets, and You have given them blood to drink. They deserve it."

7 And I heard the altar saying, "Yes, O Lord God, the Almighty, true and righteous are Your judgments."

OBSERVE

As we saw in the first lesson of this study, there are three persons in the Godhead: the Father, the Son, and the Spirit. All were involved in the creation of man. Let's see what God's Word says about the veracity—the truthfulness—of the Son and the Spirit.

ISAIAH 65:16

Because he who is blessed in the earth will be blessed by the God of truth; and he who swears in the earth will swear by the God of truth; because the former troubles are forgotten, and because they are hidden from My sight!

JOHN 1:14

And the Word [*Jesus*] became flesh, and dwelt among us, and we saw His glory, glory as of the only begotten from the Father, full of grace and truth.

JOHN 14:6

Jesus said to him, "I am the way, and the truth, and the life; no one comes to the Father but through Me."

JOHN 17:15–17

Jesus is praying to the Father just before He goes to the Garden of Gethsemane.

15 I do not ask You to take them out of the world, but to keep them from the evil one.

Leader: *Read Isaiah 65:16; John 1:14; 14:6; 17:15–17; and 16:13. Have the group…*

- *draw a triangle over the references to* **God the Father,** *including pronouns.*
- *mark the references to* **Jesus,** *including synonyms and pronouns, with a cross.*
- *draw a cloud shape like this* ⌒‿⌒ *over each reference to* **the Spirit,** *including pronouns.*
- *mark a* **T** *over each occurrence of the word* **truth.**

DISCUSS

- What do these verses teach about the Father, the Son, and the Holy Spirit in regard to truth?

INSIGHT

Truth is found in God. God is truth. This is referred to as the *veracity* of God.

• From what you see in these verses, how essential is truth to God's character? Explain your answer.

• What does the veracity of God mean to you practically? How can it impact you? Protect you? Direct you?

16 They are not of the world, even as I am not of the world.

17 Sanctify them in the truth; Your word is truth.

JOHN 16:13

But when He, the Spirit of truth, comes, He will guide you into all the truth; for He will not speak on His own initiative, but whatever He hears, He will speak; and He will disclose to you what is to come.

PSALM 119:89–91

89 Forever, O LORD, Your word is settled in heaven.

90 Your faithfulness continues throughout all generations; You established the earth, and it stands.

91 They stand this day according to Your ordinances, for all things are Your servants.

PSALM 102:25–27

25 Of old You founded the earth, and the heavens are the work of Your hands.

26 Even they will perish, but You endure; and all of them will wear out like a garment; like clothing

OBSERVE

The passages we've been studying were written millennia ago. Are they still true, given how things have changed greatly in our world, in our times? Has God changed, or will He? Let's see what God says.

Leader: Read Psalm 119:89–91; 102:25–27; 33:11; and Hebrews 13:7–8. Have the group...

- *mark the references to **the Lord,** including pronouns, with a triangle.*
- *mark the references to **Jesus,** including synonyms and pronouns, with a cross.*
- *circle all references to **time,** such as **all generations, this day,** etc.*
- *underline the entire phrase referring to **time.***

DISCUSS

- Moving through the first three passages one at a time, discuss what the group learned about the Lord from the text and the time phrases. As you do, notice the context of these truths about God.

• Can God's word be trusted? If so, for how long? How do you know? What have you learned about God that gives you the answer to these questions?

You will change them and they will be changed.

27 But You are the same, and Your years will not come to an end.

PSALM 33:11

The counsel of the LORD stands forever, the plans of His heart from generation to generation.

• What did you learn about Jesus Christ in Hebrews 13? Discuss what you observed from marking the phrase related to time.

HEBREWS 13:7–8

7 Remember those who led you, who spoke the word of God to you; and considering the result of their conduct, imitate their faith.

8 Jesus Christ is the same yesterday and today and forever.

- The unchanging nature of God is known as His *immutability.* (See Insight box.) How can knowing this attribute of God help you in a practical way?

INSIGHT

God is *immutable.* This means God is always the same in His nature, His character, and His will. He never changes, and He can never be made to change. And because the Bible is the Word of God, it will never change. Immutability is an attribute of God that assures you He can be trusted forever and ever.

- If possible, spend some time as a group thanking God for what you've learned about Him in this week's study. Remember God inhabits the praises of His people (Psalm 22:3).

WRAP IT UP

Are you awed with God? Stunned by all you are learning for yourself about Him? It makes such a difference when you allow God to speak for Himself, when you listen to His Word directly rather than to the opinions of others. It helps to know what God says so you can measure what man says against the plumbline of His Word.

The question then becomes, who will you believe? What will direct and order your life, your thinking, your behavior, your attitude?

You have looked at enough verses from various books of the Bible to see that God is righteous and just in all His ways. Righteousness and justice are the foundation of His throne; therefore all that our sovereign God does is right and just. Lovingkindness and truth go before Him.

If you will get to know His Word and watch God in action and genuinely listen to what He says, then you will know right from wrong, truth from lies, and know how you are to live. You will gain strength and courage—courage to trust God, to obey Him no matter the circumstances.

And with that will come an inner peace that you cannot find any place else. It is found solely in knowing God, in the assurance of His absolute veracity and His immutability. Because the Lord God will never change, you can stake everything on Him.

But, you may ask, *how does God feel about me? Because He is omnipresent and omniscient, I know He knows all about me; will this make a difference in the way He treats me?*

Remember His lovingkindness—His grace, His favor is always

making the way, going before Him to you. That is what we will explore in our next lesson—a lesson you won't want to miss.

Until then, why don't you make it a point each day to thank God for one thing you have learned about Him in these four lessons. You might also want to keep a journal, even recording just a line or two each day about how these truths of God are shaping your decisions, direction, relationships, and well-being.

We've learned much about the character and ways of God in the past four lessons. We've seen that He's the self-existent, self-sufficient Creator. He is the righteous, just, all-powerful, all-knowing, all-present Sovereign who rules over all. A God of truth who never changes.

As we've delved into His Word, we've also caught a glimpse of His wrath—an aspect of God that many dislike and others doubt! In light of this, we want to know whether this great and awesome Sovereign loves us. And if not, how can we get Him to love us—especially when He knows the truth of what we are like?

In this lesson we will explore what God tells us of His love.

Get prepared to experience His character in a way that should capture your heart. In fact, why don't you pause as a group and ask God to reveal Himself to you—to show each of you where you stand with Him.

OBSERVE

Those who haven't studied the full Word of God for themselves often think that the God of the Old Testament is different from the God of the New Testament. The God of the Old Testament seems to them an angry, wrathful deity who is somehow tempered by the time of Jesus so that He becomes more compassionate and loving. By now you know that cannot be true, because you have seen that God is immutable. He does not change.

So let's see for ourselves what place love has in the nature of God, starting with an encounter between God and Moses, in which the Lord answered Moses' request to "show me Your glory" (Exodus 33:18).

EXODUS 34:6–7

⁶ Then the LORD passed by in front of him [*Moses*] and proclaimed, "The LORD, the LORD God, compassionate and gracious, slow to anger, and abounding in lovingkindness and truth;

⁷ who keeps lovingkindness for thousands, who forgives iniquity, transgression and sin; yet He will by no means leave the guilty unpunished, visiting the iniquity of fathers on the children and on the grandchildren to the third and fourth generations."

Leader: Read Exodus 34:6–7. Have the group...

- *draw a triangle over the references to **the Lord**, including pronouns:* △
- *mark each occurrence of the word **lovingkindness** with a heart, like this:* ♡

DISCUSS

- How is God described in these verses? Don't miss a thing He tells you about Himself in this account of His revelation to Moses.

- What did you learn from marking *lovingkindness*?

INSIGHT

Lovingkindness, the translation of the Hebrew word *hesed*, speaks of grace and favor. *Hesed* is used often in respect to the covenant relationship between God and Israel.

OBSERVE

In these next verses, we read what Moses said to the children of Israel as they were getting ready to go into the land God had promised them as an everlasting possession. By the way, they had just finished wandering in the wilderness for forty years because they wouldn't trust God even after He redeemed them from slavery in Egypt!

Leader: Read Deuteronomy 7:6–10. Have the group…

- put a triangle over every reference to **the Lord,** including pronouns.
- mark each occurrence of the words **love** and **lovingkindness** with a heart.

DISCUSS

- What did you learn from marking *love* and *lovingkindness*?

DEUTERONOMY 7:6–10

6 For you are a holy people to the LORD your God; the LORD your God has chosen you to be a people for His own possession out of all the peoples who are on the face of the earth.

7 The LORD did not set His love on you nor choose you because you were more in number than any of the peoples, for you were the fewest of all peoples,

8 but because the LORD loved you and kept the oath which He swore to your fore-fathers, the LORD brought you out by a mighty hand and redeemed you from

the house of slavery, from the hand of Pharaoh king of Egypt.

9 Know therefore that the LORD your God, He is God, the faithful God, who keeps His covenant and His lovingkindness to a thousandth generation with those who love Him and keep His commandments;

10 but repays those who hate Him to their faces, to destroy them; He will not delay with him who hates Him, He will repay him to his face.

- What contrast is being made between verses 9 and 10?

- What did you learn about God from verses 9–10?

- Is this fair? Why or why not?

- How do the truths in this passage line up with what you've learned about God in the previous four lessons?

OBSERVE

We've seen God's declaration of His love for Israel. How long will it last? These are obstinate and rebellious people—a fact you will see for yourself when you read through the Old Testament. The following verses speak of Israel's restoration after judgment for their sins.

Leader: Read Jeremiah 31:1–3 and Micah 7:18. Have the group…

- *circle every reference to **the families, the people of Israel**.*
- *put a triangle over the references to **the Lord**.*
- *draw a heart over every reference to **love** or **lovingkindness**.*

DISCUSS

- What did you learn from the text about God's relationship with His chosen people?

- How long will His love last? Why?

JEREMIAH 31:1–3

¹ "At that time," declares the LORD, "I will be the God of all the families of Israel, and they shall be My people."

² Thus says the LORD, "The people who survived the sword found grace in the wilderness—Israel, when it went to find its rest."

³ The LORD appeared to him [*Israel*] from afar, saying, "I have loved you with an everlasting love; therefore I have drawn you with lovingkindness."

MICAH 7:18

Who is a God like You, who pardons iniquity and passes over the rebellious act of the remnant of His possession? He does not retain His anger forever, because He delights in unchanging love.

1 JOHN 4:9–10, 16, 19

9 By this the love of God was manifested in us, that God has sent His only begotten Son into the world so that we might live through Him.

10 In this is love, not that we loved God, but that He loved us and sent His Son to be the propitiation for our sins....

16 We have come to know and have believed the love which God has for us. God is love, and the

• In contrast, how long will His anger last?

OBSERVE

Let's look at some New Testament passages that further reveal the nature of God's love.

Leader: Read 1 John 4:9–10, 16, 19 and John 3:16–17, 35–36 aloud. Have the group do the following:
- *Mark the references to **God** with a triangle.*
- *Mark the references to **the Son, Jesus Christ,** with a cross. Don't miss any pronouns!*
- *Draw a heart over every occurrence of **love** or **loved**.*
- *Mark the word **wrath** with a **W.***

DISCUSS

• What did you learn from marking *God*?

• What did you learn from marking the references to the Son of God, Jesus Christ?

• According to these verses, how can you know God loves you?

• What happens to those who believe in Jesus?

• What happens to those who do not obey Him—who do not believe that He is the Son of God who died so that we would not perish?

one who abides in love abides in God, and God abides in him....

19 We love, because He first loved us.

JOHN 3:16–17, 35–36

16 For God so loved the world, that He gave His only begotten Son, that whoever believes in Him shall not perish, but have eternal life.

17 For God did not send the Son into the world to judge the world, but that the world might be saved through Him....

35 The Father loves the Son and has given all things into His hand.

36 He who believes in the Son has eternal life; but he who does not obey the Son will not see life, but the wrath of God abides on him.

EPHESIANS 2:4–5

4 But God, being rich in mercy, because of His great love with which He loved us,

5 even when we were dead in our transgressions, made us alive together with Christ (by grace you have been saved).

ROMAN 5:6–10

6 For while we were still helpless, at the right time Christ died for the ungodly.

• Is it fair of God to do this? Explain your answer.

OBSERVE

Those who don't know or study the Word of God believe that God cannot love them until they straighten their lives out, until they get themselves cleaned up, so to speak. Let's see what God says.

Leader: Read Ephesians 2:4–5 and Romans 5:6–10 aloud. Have the group…
- *circle every reference to **people,** however they are described, including pronouns.*
- *put a triangle over **God.***
- *put a cross over every reference to **Christ.***
- *mark **wrath** with a **W.***

DISCUSS

- What did God and Jesus do to show their love for us?

- What was our condition when God did this?

- What does this reveal about God?

- So do people have to get their lives cleaned up, straightened out so that God will love them? How do you know?

7 For one will hardly die for a righteous man; though perhaps for the good man someone would dare even to die.

8 But God demonstrates His own love toward us, in that while we were yet sinners, Christ died for us.

9 Much more then, having now been justified by His blood, we shall be saved from the wrath of God through Him.

10 For if while we were enemies we were reconciled to God through the death of His Son, much more, having been reconciled, we shall be saved by His life.

ROMANS 8:31–32, 35, 37–39

31 What then shall we say to these things? If God is for us, who is against us?

32 He who did not spare His own Son, but delivered Him over for us all, how will He not also with Him freely give us all things?...

35 Who will separate us from the love of Christ? Will tribulation, or distress, or persecution, or famine, or nakedness, or peril, or sword?...

37 But in all these things we overwhelmingly conquer through Him who loved us.

38 For I am convinced that neither

OBSERVE

Sometimes when Christians undergo trials and hardships, or things don't go well, they think God doesn't love them. Is this true? Can those who believe in Jesus—those who receive Him as their Lord and God—expect life to be free of trouble?

Leader: Read Romans 8:31–32, 35, 37–39 aloud. Have the group do the following:

- *Mark every reference to **God** with a triangle.*
- *Put a cross over every reference to **Jesus Christ, God's Son.***
- *Circle every reference to **believers,** including the pronouns **us** and **we.***
- *Draw a heart over every occurrence of **love** or **loved.***

DISCUSS

- What did you learn from marking the references to those who belong to Christ?

• What holds true for all believers, no matter their circumstances?

• How would knowing the truths of these verses help you in difficulties?

OBSERVE

Leader: Read 1 John 5:2–3 and John 13:34–35 and have the group…

  • *circle every **we** and **you**.*
  • *draw a heart over **love** and **loved**.*

DISCUSS

• Now, what responsibility does being loved by God bring to a true believer?

death, nor life, nor angels, nor principalities, nor things present, nor things to come, nor powers,

39 nor height, nor depth, nor any other created thing, will be able to separate us from the love of God, which is in Christ Jesus our Lord.

1 John 5:2–3

2 By this we know that we love the children of God, when we love God and observe His commandments.

3 For this is the love of God, that we keep His commandments; and His commandments are not burdensome.

JOHN 13:34–35

Jesus is speaking:

34 A new commandment I give to you, that you love one another, even as I have loved you, that you also love one another.

35 By this all men will know that you are My disciples, if you have love for one another.

1 JOHN 3:14–19

14 We know that we have passed out of death into life, because we love the brethren. He who does not love abides in death.

15 Everyone who hates his brother is a murderer; and you know that no murderer has eternal life abiding in him.

• What will be the result when we fulfill that responsibility?

OBSERVE

Is love more than just a word you say to another? How does love look in human flesh?

Leader: Read 1 John 3:14–19 aloud. Have the group...

> • *circle every reference to **people,** however they are described, including pronouns like **we** and **us.***
>
> • *draw a heart over every occurrence of **love** and **heart.***
>
> • *mark a **T** over each occurrence of the word **truth.***

DISCUSS

• What did you learn from marking the references to the people?

• What shows that we love?

• What does this passage reveal about the one who says "I love God" yet hates his brother?

• How exactly should we show love to others, according to verses 17–18?

16 We know love by this, that He laid down His life for us; and we ought to lay down our lives for the brethren.

17 But whoever has the world's goods, and sees his brother in need and closes his heart against him, how does the love of God abide in him?

18 Little children, let us not love with word or with tongue, but in deed and truth.

19 We will know by this that we are of the truth, and will assure our heart before Him.

4 Love is patient, love is kind and is not jealous; love does not brag and is not arrogant,

5 does not act unbecomingly; it does not seek its own, is not provoked, does not take into account a wrong suffered,

6 does not rejoice in unrighteousness, but rejoices with the truth;

7 bears all things, believes all things, hopes all things, endures all things.

8 Love never fails.

OBSERVE

Leader: Read 1 Corinthians 13:4–8.

> • *Have the group underline each word or phrase that* ***describes love.***

DISCUSS

• According to these verses in 1 Corinthians 13, how do we show love in deed and truth? Be as specific and practical as you can.

• Think through the truths about the love of God that you've seen in this lesson. Summarize what God says happens to us when we experience the love of God by believing in Jesus Christ.

• Second Corinthians 13:5 tells us, "Test yourselves to see if you are in the faith; examine yourselves!" Take time now to do that. It would be the worst mistake of your life to think you are a Christian if you are not! So ask yourself whether you are a true Christian and how you know it. What is the evidence?

WRAP IT UP

"How great a love the Father has bestowed on us, that we would be called children of God; and such we are" (1 John 3:1).

Oh beloved of God, stop and think about what you've learned about the love of God this week. Go back through the words of God you've just studied. Meditate on them, let them fill your mind, saturate your heart, go deep into your soul—your inner man. You are loved unconditionally, eternally, with an everlasting love. He called you "Beloved" when there was nothing lovely about you.

Once you come to God, acknowledging your sin, your impotence to save yourself, your need of a Savior, His love will be poured out in your heart through the Spirit of God who He gives to you. Once you truly believe, once you truly receive Jesus, nothing—absolutely nothing!—will ever be able to separate you from His everlasting love. You are a member of God's forever family. Let this truth go deep into your soul until it's absorbed by every fiber of your being.

God holds you in His hand. No one can take you out of this hand. Everything that comes into your life will be filtered through His sovereign fingers of love. Think about it, beloved. Isn't that reassuring? As His child, nothing that happens in your life will ever be more than you can bear. This is your spiritual birthright.

The more secure you become in His love, the more you will find yourself freely loving others with the love of God—even your enemies. And by this others will know that you are a true disciple of Jesus Christ.*

If you have the time, it would be so good to worship God, thanking Him for His great love with which He has loved you (Ephesians 2:4).

---

* To learn more about how to love in deed and in truth, we recommend the 40–Minute Bible study *Loving God, Loving Others.*

"God is good. All the time God is good. Why? Because that is His nature!" You'll hear this or similar words in many Christian gatherings as believers remind themselves of this attribute of God. In one of his psalms David urged us to "taste and see that the LORD is good" (Psalm 34:8). The goodness of God is seen in His mercy, His compassion, His grace, His faithfulness—all attributes of God's character that set Him apart as God. We have not had time to explore them, but you will see these characteristics as you study God's Word for yourself. Along with His lovingkindness, these are attributes that we love, that are easy to accept because they are what we want God to be.

But what about God's wrath? What about His holiness? What about His jealousy? These are three critical attributes of God that we will explore this week. Each of these is just as essential to His nature as lovingkindness, so we need to understand what these characteristics mean for our relationship with Him. It's going to be an enlightening and, believe it or not, a liberating way to bring our study to a close.

OBSERVE

As we studied the love of God, you were asked to mark two references to the wrath of God. Let's look at these scriptures again and see what we learn.

JOHN 3:36

He who believes in the Son has eternal life; but he who does not obey the Son will not see life, but the wrath of God abides on him.

ROMANS 5:8–9

8 But God demonstrates His own love toward us, in that while we were yet sinners, Christ died for us.

9 Much more then, having now been justified by His blood, we shall be saved from the wrath of God through Him.

2 KINGS 22:11, 13

While cleaning out the temple of God, the people of Judah found the Torah, the first five books of the Bible, which are also called the Law. This is the setting of these verses.

Leader: Read John 3:36 and Romans 5:8–9 aloud and have the group…

- *mark **wrath** with a **W.***
- *circle the pronouns **he, him, us, we.***

DISCUSS

- What did you learn from marking *wrath*?

- Whose wrath is described in these verses?

- What provokes the wrath? Does this seem fair?

- How does a person escape this wrath?

OBSERVE

People often think of the "Old Testament God" as a God of wrath, yet you have just seen God's wrath active in the New Testament. Wrath comes because of unbelief and disobedience, any act that is contrary to the will of God. Let's compare an Old Testament passage with several New Testament passages and see what we learn from them about the wrath of God.

Leader: *Read aloud 2 Kings 22:11, 13; Romans 1:16–19; 2:2–8; and 1 Thessalonians 1:9–10.*

> • *Have the group mark **wrath** and **judgment** with a **W.***

DISCUSS

• Look at each passage and discuss what you learned from marking *wrath* and *judgment*.

11 When the king heard the words of the book of the law, he tore his clothes.…

13 "Go, inquire of the LORD for me and the people and all Judah concerning the words of this book that has been found, for great is the wrath of the LORD that burns against us, because our fathers have not listened to the words of this book, to do according to all that is written concerning us."

ROMANS 1:16–19

16 For I am not ashamed of the gospel, for it is the power of God for salvation to everyone who believes, to the Jew first and also to the Greek.

17 For in it the righteousness of God is revealed from faith to faith; as it is written, "But the righteous man shall live by faith."

18 For the wrath of God is revealed from heaven against all ungodliness and unrighteousness of men who suppress the truth in unrighteousness,

19 because that which is known about God is evident within them; for God made it evident to them.

ROMANS 2:2–8

2 And we know that the judgment of God rightly falls upon those who practice such things.

INSIGHT

The verb *revealed* in Romans 1:18 is in the present tense, which implies continuous action.

• What reasons are given for the wrath, or judgment, of God? Don't miss a single one.

• Who is affected by God's judgment, His wrath?

• When and how is God's wrath or judgment experienced?

3 But do you suppose this, O man, when you pass judgment on those who practice such things and do the same yourself, that you will escape the judgment of God?

4 Or do you think lightly of the riches of His kindness and tolerance and patience, not knowing that the kindness of God leads you to repentance?

5 But because of your stubbornness and unrepentant heart you are storing up wrath for yourself in the day of wrath and revelation of the righteous judgment of God,

6 who will render to each person according to his deeds:

7 to those who by perseverance in doing good seek for glory and honor and immortality, eternal life;

8 but to those who are selfishly ambitious and do not obey the truth, but obey unrighteousness, wrath and indignation.

1 THESSALONIANS 1:9–10

9 For they themselves report about us what kind of a reception we had with you, and how you turned to God from idols to serve a living and true God,

10 and to wait for His Son from heaven, whom He raised from the dead, that is Jesus, who rescues us from the wrath to come.

• What did you learn about God from these passages?

OBSERVE

How important is it for us to understand the wrath of God and the reason for His wrath?

Leader: Read Ephesians 5:3–6 aloud. Have the group do the following:

- *Circle every occurrence of **you**.*
- *Underline every **behavior** that is mentioned in these verses.*
- *Mark the phrases **you know with certainty** and **let no one deceive** with a check mark, like this: ✓*
- *Mark **wrath** with a **W**.*

DISCUSS

- What did you learn from marking *wrath*?

- Move carefully through the passage verse by verse and discuss what God tells us about people who engage in the behaviors listed.

EPHESIANS 5:3–6

3 But immorality or any impurity or greed must not even be named among you, as is proper among saints;

4 and there must be no filthiness and silly talk, or coarse jesting, which are not fitting, but rather giving of thanks.

5 For this you know with certainty, that no immoral or impure person or covetous man, who is an idolater, has an inheritance in the kingdom of Christ and God.

6 Let no one deceive you with empty words, for because of these

things the wrath of God comes upon the sons of disobedience.

• How are these people described in verse 6?

• What did you learn from marking *know with certainty* and *let no one deceive you*? What does this tell you about the importance of what Paul was writing under the inspiration of God?

• What responsibility, if any, do you have in regard to people who claim to be believers but are participating in these things?

2 THESSALONIANS 1:6–10

6 For after all it is only just for God to repay with affliction those who afflict you,

7 and to give relief to you who are afflicted and to us as well when the Lord Jesus will be revealed from heaven with His mighty angels in flaming fire,

OBSERVE

Living righteously, according to the Word of God and the character of God, can and will bring suffering and affliction. Will those who persecute believers and live unrighteously get away with it?

Leader: Read 2 Thessalonians 1:6–10 aloud. Have the group do the following:
- *Mark every reference to **God** with a triangle.*
- *Put a cross over every reference to **Jesus**.*
- *Circle every **you** and **us** that refers to **believers**, including the synonym **saints**.*

- *Mark the word **afflict** in all its forms like this:* ⚡

DISCUSS

- What did you see when you marked *God* and *Jesus*? What can we expect them to do in the future?

- What did you learn from marking the references to the believers?

- Although the word *wrath* is not found in this passage, did you see any evidence of God's wrath?

Leader: *Read through the passage again and have the group put a **W** over any word or phrase that the group thinks shows God's wrath. Then discuss what they observed.*

- Now that you are aware of the wrath of God, you will be alert to its presence in many verses throughout the Bible. The question is, how do you feel about this aspect of God's nature—and why?

8 dealing out retribution to those who do not know God and to those who do not obey the gospel of our Lord Jesus.

9 These will pay the penalty of eternal destruction, away from the presence of the Lord and from the glory of His power,

10 when He comes to be glorified in His saints on that day, and to be marveled at among all who have believed—for our testimony to you was believed.

OBSERVE

Wrath is God's response to sin in all its forms. His righteousness, His justice, His holiness command His just judgment against all that would harm an individual and destroy mankind. Thus His wrath. We have looked at God's righteousness and His justice, but we have not yet explored His holiness. We will do that next, beginning with one verse from a song Moses sang to the Lord after God parted the Red Sea and delivered the children of Israel from the army of Pharaoh. The waters separated, the Israelites went across the sea on dry ground, then God drowned the pursuing Pharaoh and his Egyptian army in the same sea!

Leader: *Read Exodus 15:11 aloud as a group.*

- *Have the group mark **holiness** with a cloud, like this:*

EXODUS 15:11

Who is like You among the gods, O LORD? Who is like You, majestic in holiness, awesome in praises, working wonders?

INSIGHT

The biblical concept of *holiness* is difficult to define in a few words, but it contains the idea of *being separate.* It suggests a separation between what is pure and what is unclean. God is separate from all that is evil or defiled. His character is the standard for moral perfection.

The words *holy* and *holiness* are used approximately seven hundred times in the Bible. The concept first appears in Exodus 3, where God appears to Moses in a burning bush. God declares the place "holy ground" and tells Moses to take off his shoes. Thus you see the concept of separation.

The idea of separation, being set apart for God, is affirmed over and over again in referring to assemblies, garments, days, oil, and even the Holy of Holies in the temple. Only one piece of furniture was put in the Holy of Holies, the ark of the covenant, which represented the throne of God.

DISCUSS

• What does Exodus 15:11 tell you about God?

• Reviewing the events that preceded this, can you understand why these words were included in the song?

• What do you think "majestic in holiness" means?

LEVITICUS 10:1–3

Now Nadab and Abihu, the sons of Aaron, took their respective firepans, and after putting fire in them, placed incense on it and offered strange fire before the LORD, which He had not commanded them.

² And fire came out from the presence of

OBSERVE

Next we'll see God's holiness in action. Hang on! It's quite a story. Aaron was the high priest and his sons served with him in the tabernacle. God ordered a daily sacrifice for which incense of a very precise formula was to be burned in the holy place on the altar of incense. This altar was in front of the veil leading to the Holy of Holies.

Leader: Read Leviticus 10:1–3 aloud. Have the group…

> • *mark every reference to **the Lord,** including pronouns, with a triangle.*
> • *draw a cloud around the word **holy.***

DISCUSS

• Briefly summarize the events described in these three verses.

• How did this story affect you?

• What did you learn about the Lord? About the gravity of God's holiness?

• In the light of all you've learned about God's character, how would you explain God's actions?

OBSERVE

What does God expect from His people?

Leader: Read Leviticus 11:44–45 aloud and have the group…
> • *mark each reference to **the Lord** with a triangle.*
> • *circle every occurrence of **you, your,** and **yourselves.***
> • *draw a cloud around the word **holy.***

the LORD and consumed them, and they died before the LORD.

3 Then Moses said to Aaron, "It is what the LORD spoke, saying, 'By those who come near Me I will be treated as holy, and before all the people I will be honored.' " So Aaron, therefore, kept silent.

LEVITICUS 11:44–45

God is speaking to the children of Israel.

44 For I am the LORD your God. Consecrate yourselves therefore, and be holy, for I am holy. And you shall not make yourselves unclean with any of the swarming things that swarm on the earth.

45 For I am the LORD who brought you up from the land of Egypt to be your God; thus you shall be holy, for I am holy.

ISAIAH 6:1–5

1 In the year of King Uzziah's death I saw the Lord sitting on a throne, lofty and exalted, with the train of His robe filling the temple.

2 Seraphim stood above Him, each having six wings: with two he covered his face, and with two he covered his feet, and with two he flew.

3 And one called out to another and said, "Holy, Holy, Holy, is the LORD of hosts, the

DISCUSS

• What were the Lord's instructions and what reason(s) did He give?

• How is holiness demonstrated in this passage?

OBSERVE

How does one respond to the presence of a holy God?

Leader: Read Isaiah 6:1–5 aloud and have the group...

> • *put a triangle over every reference to* **the Lord,** *including the pronouns* **His** *and* **Him.**
> • *circle all references to* **Isaiah,** *the one speaking in this passage.*

DISCUSS

• What did you learn about the Lord in this passage?

- What happened to Isaiah when he saw the Lord—and why?

- Discuss what you've observed about most people's understanding of or response to God's holiness.

- Do you think that those who claim to be Christians truly understand the holiness of the Lord and live their lives accordingly?

- What about you? How are these verses speaking to you?

whole earth is full of His glory."

4 And the foundations of the thresholds trembled at the voice of him who called out, while the temple was filling with smoke.

5 Then I said, "Woe is me, for I am ruined!

6 Because I am a man of unclean lips, and I live among a people of unclean lips; for my eyes have seen the King, the LORD of hosts."

1 Peter 1:14–16

14 As obedient children, do not be conformed to the former lusts which were yours in your ignorance,

15 but like the Holy One who called you, be holy yourselves also in all your behavior;

16 because it is written, "You shall be holy, for I am holy."

1 Peter 2:9–12

9 But you are a chosen race, a royal priesthood, a holy nation, a people for God's own possession, so that you may proclaim the excellencies of Him who has called you out of darkness into His marvelous light;

OBSERVE

God told the nation of Israel that they were to be holy. What about those of us who claim to be Christians?

Leader: Read 1 Peter 1:14–16 and 2:9–12. Have the group…

- *circle every reference to **believers**, including pronouns and synonyms, such as **obedient children**.*
- *put a triangle over each reference to **God**, including pronouns and synonyms such as **the Holy One**.*
- *draw a cloud around each occurrence of the word **holy**.*

DISCUSS

- What did you learn about believers from these two passages?

• Describe how we are to behave, and why.

10 for you once were not a people, but now you are the people of God; you had not received mercy, but now you have received mercy.

11 Beloved, I urge you as aliens and strangers to abstain from fleshly lusts which wage war against the soul.

• Is that possible, or is God expecting too much of us, given the culture in which we live? Explain your answer.

12 Keep your behavior excellent among the Gentiles, so that in the thing in which they slander you as evildoers, they may because of your good deeds, as they observe them, glorify God in the day of visitation.

1 CORINTHIANS 6:19–20

19 Or do you not know that your body is a temple of the Holy Spirit who is in you, whom you have from God, and that you are not your own?

20 For you have been bought with a price: therefore glorify God in your body.

GALATIANS 5:16–18

16 But I say, walk by the Spirit, and you will not carry out the desire of the flesh.

17 For the flesh sets its desire against the Spirit, and the Spirit against the flesh; for these are in opposition to one another, so that you may not do the things that you please.

OBSERVE

How is it possible to be holy as God is holy? Let's see what the apostle Paul wrote to a minority group of believers who lived in a culture that was as immoral, as licentious as our culture.

Leader: Read 1 Corinthians 6:19–20 and Galatians 5:16–18 aloud. Have the group…
- *circle each **you** and **your**.*
- *put an **S** over the references to **the Spirit**.*
- *put an **F** over the references to **the flesh**.*

DISCUSS

- Look at the passages one by one. First, what did you learn from marking *you* and *your* in 1 Corinthians 6:19–20?

- What question is presented to believers?

- What is the price that was paid to save you? (We looked at it in the lesson on God's love.)

- If the Holy Spirit is in you, what difference does that make in your ability to be holy?

- Now, what did you learn from marking *you* in Galatians 5? Don't miss a thing.

- What did you learn from marking *the Spirit* in both passages?

- Compare the flesh and the Spirit. What do you learn?

- What have you learned that can help you be holy even as God is holy?

- Think about Galatians 5:18. What God wants you to know is that you are made holy by the indwelling Holy Spirit, not by trying to keep the law. Remember that: holiness comes from yielding to the Spirit rather than trying to control your flesh by a list of do's and don'ts!

18 But if you are led by the Spirit, you are not under the Law.

Exodus 20:2–6

2 I am the LORD your God, who brought you out of the land of Egypt, out of the house of slavery.

3 You shall have no other gods before Me.

4 You shall not make for yourself an idol, or any likeness of what is in heaven above or on the earth beneath or in the water under the earth.

5 You shall not worship them or serve them; for I, the LORD your God, am a jealous God, visiting the iniquity of the fathers on the children, on the third and the fourth generations of those who hate Me,

OBSERVE

In a study like this we don't have time to look at every attribute of God. However, there is one final attribute we want to consider before we close our study.

Leader: Read Exodus 20:2–6 and 34:12–14 aloud. Have the group…
- *put a triangle over every reference to **God**, including pronouns and synonyms.*
- *circle each **you** and **your**.*
- *mark every reference to **idols**—anything worshipped, bowed to other than God—with a big **I**.*

DISCUSS

- What does God tell you about Himself in these two passages? What kind of a God is He?

• What will God do because of who He is?

INSIGHT

It is important to understand the difference between jealousy and envy. *Envy* is wishing you had something someone else has. *Jealousy* is not wanting someone else to have what you have.

• Considering all you have learned about God from His Word, is God's jealousy good or bad? Explain your answer.

6 but showing lovingkindness to thousands, to those who love Me and keep My commandments.

Exodus 34:12–14

12 Watch yourself that you make no covenant with the inhabitants of the land into which you are going, or it will become a snare in your midst.

13 But rather, you are to tear down their altars and smash their sacred pillars and cut down their Asherim

14 —for you shall not worship any other god, for the LORD, whose name is Jealous, is a jealous God.

2 CORINTHIANS 6:14, 16–7:1

14 Do not be bound [*unequally yoked*] together with unbelievers; for what partnership have righteousness and lawlessness, or what fellowship has light with darkness?....

16 Or what agreement has the temple of God with idols? For we are the temple of the living God; just as God said, "I will dwell in them and walk among them; and I will be their God, and they shall be my people.

17 "Therefore, come out from their midst and be separate," says the Lord. "And do not touch what is unclean; and I will welcome you.

OBSERVE

So what are God's instructions to us who have His Spirit living in us?

Leader: Read 2 Corinthians 6:14,16–7:1 and Colossians 3:5–6, 9–10 aloud. Have the group...

- *put a triangle over every reference to* **God.**
- *circle each pronoun referring to* **believers,** *such as* **we, them,** *and* **you.**
- *mark every reference to* **idols** *and* **idolatry** *with an* **I.**

DISCUSS

- What did you learn about believers in these passages?

• Did you see the word *holiness* in 2 Corinthians 7:1? How does it apply to believers and what do you think it means practically?

• According to these verses in 2 Corinthians 6 and 7, how is holiness accomplished?

• What did you learn about idolatry in these passages?

18 "And I will be a father to you, and you shall be sons and daughters to Me," says the Lord Almighty.

7:1 Therefore, having these promises, beloved, let us cleanse ourselves from all defilement of flesh and spirit, perfecting holiness in the fear of God.

COLOSSIANS 3:5–6, 9–10

5 Therefore consider the members of your earthly body as dead to immorality, impurity, passion, evil desire, and greed, which amounts to idolatry.

6 For it is because of these things that the wrath of God will come upon the sons of disobedience....

⁹ Do not lie to one another, since you laid aside the old self with its evil practices,

¹⁰ and have put on the new self who is being renewed to a true knowledge according to the image of the One who created him.

• What is described as idolatry in Colossians 3:5?

INSIGHT

God has much to say in His Word with respect to idols and their worship. An idol is anything that you bow down to, that you put in the rightful place of God, anything that receives a priority over Him in your affections. An idol is a counterfeit god that will lead you away from loving God with all your heart, mind, soul, body, and strength. God does not tolerate idols, and He knows how to remove them. They are bad for you; they keep you from being all that God, in His goodness, desires for you and for His kingdom.

God is jealous. He is jealous for your holiness—your sanctification— without which, He says, "no one will see the Lord" (Hebrews 12:14).

• Do you think idolatry is a problem today among God's people? Explain your answer.

• What do we need to do in light of what you've seen?

• Read Colossians 3:10 aloud once more, then think about the knowledge you've gained about God—true knowledge because you saw it in His Word. How has and will such knowledge affect you?

WRAP IT UP

In Colossians 3:10, the believer is described as having "put on the new self who is being renewed to a true knowledge according to the image of the One who created him"! This takes us back to where we began—in Genesis, the book of beginnings where we first met God as Creator. What an awesome thought to bring our study to a close, beloved of God. (You know now, don't you, that you are beloved of God and it is good and right to remind you of this?)

If you have listened to God, you know that when the Father, Son, and Holy Spirit first created us, male and female, they created us in their image. Although that image was marred, distorted, cut off from God because of the sin of unbelief and disobedience, we have hope of its restoration. Because God is love, He called us beloved when there was nothing lovely about us. Out of love, grace, mercy, and kindness the eternal Father justly redeemed us through the life, death, burial, and resurrection of the Holy Son of God, our Lord Jesus Christ.

Greater love has never been known, never been seen in that while we were sinners, without hope, helpless, ungodly—literally enemies of God—Christ Jesus, the only begotten Son of God, died for us. He took on our sin, even though the wages of sin is death, and paid for it in full. And because God's holiness was satisfied (propitiated), He raised Him from the dead, never to die again. Thus when we believe in the name of Jesus we pass from death to life—everlasting life.

And because God is sovereign—because all is under the dominion of the Most High God—you and I have the absolute assurance that "God causes all things to work together for good to those who love

God" (Romans 8:28). To those who, convicted of their sin, repent and accept Jesus, God in the flesh, as our Savior, our Lord. We have been called by God, chosen in Him before the foundation of the world, according to God's eternal purpose. God foreknew us, predestined us, marked out beforehand for us "to become conformed to the image of His Son" (Romans 8:29).

It is breathtaking…awe-inspiring…humbling that, as we grow in "the true knowledge of Him who called us by His own glory and excellence" (2 Peter 1:3), we become more and more like Him. Strengthened, able to be courageous, to actively serve Him wherever and however He in His omniscience desires us to live until He calls us home.

Home! Heaven! Jesus is there now, in His Father's home, preparing a place for us. Soon He will return to take us there. Or, if we die first, then we will be with Him when He returns in all His glory to rule and reign as King of kings and Lord of lords.

Oh beloved of the Father, walk by the Holy Spirit. Don't give Him the slightest cause for jealousy. Be holy as He is holy, so that when you see the Holy One you'll hear Him declare, "Well done, good and faithful servant.… Enter into the joy of your master!" (Matthew 25:21, ESV).

Now to the King eternal, immortal, invisible, the only God,
be honor and glory forever and ever. Amen. (1 Timothy 1:17)

40 MINUTE BIBLE STUDIES

No-Homework
That Help You

A 6-WEEK, NO-HOMEWORK BIBLE STUDY
MORE THAN 700,000 SOLD IN THE SERIES

Being a Disciple:
Counting the
Real Cost

Kay Arthur, Tom & Jane Hart

PRECEPT MINISTRIES INTERNATIONAL

40minute BIBLE STUDY

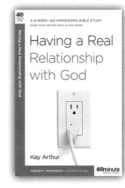

A 6-WEEK, NO-HOMEWORK BIBLE STUDY
MORE THAN 700,000 SOLD IN THE SERIES

Having a Real
Relationship
with God

Kay Arthur

PRECEPT MINISTRIES INTERNATIONAL

40minute BIBLE STUDY

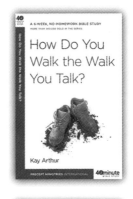

A 6-WEEK, NO-HOMEWORK BIBLE STUDY

How Do You
Walk the Walk
You Talk?

Kay Arthur

40minute BIBLE STUDY

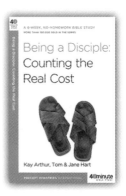

A 6-WEEK, NO-HOMEWORK BIBLE STUDY
MORE THAN 700,000 SOLD IN THE SERIES

Living a
Life of
True Worship

Kay Arthur, Bob & Diane Vereen

PRECEPT MINISTRIES INTERNATIONAL

40minute BIBLE STUDY

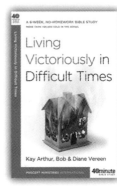

A 6-WEEK, NO-HOMEWORK BIBLE STUDY
MORE THAN 700,000 SOLD IN THE SERIES

Living
Victoriously in
Difficult Times

Kay Arthur, Bob & Diane Vereen

40minute BIBLE STUDY

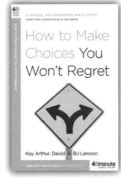

A 6-WEEK, NO-HOMEWORK BIBLE STUDY
MORE THAN 700,000 SOLD IN THE SERIES

How to Make
Choices You
Won't Regret

Kay Arthur, David & BJ Lawson

PRECEPT MINISTRIES INTERNATIONAL

40minute BIBLE STUDY

A 6-WEEK, NO-HOMEWORK BIBLE STUDY
MORE THAN 700,000 SOLD IN THE SERIES

Money and
Possessions:
The Quest for
Contentment

Kay Arthur & David Arthur

40minute BIBLE STUDY

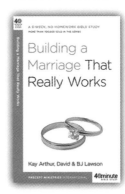

A 6-WEEK, NO-HOMEWORK BIBLE STUDY
MORE THAN 700,000 SOLD IN THE SERIES

Building a
Marriage That
Really Works

Kay Arthur, David & BJ Lawson

PRECEPT MINISTRIES INTERNATIONAL

40minute BIBLE STUDY

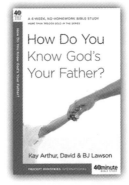

A 6-WEEK, NO-HOMEWORK BIBLE STUDY
MORE THAN 700,000 SOLD IN THE SERIES

How Do You
Know God's
Your Father?

Kay Arthur, David & BJ Lawson

PRECEPT MINISTRIES INTERNATIONAL

40minute BIBLE STUDY

Bible Studies
Discover Truth For Yourself

Discovering What the Future Holds

Kay Arthur & Georg Huber

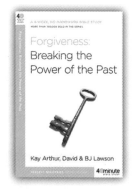

Forgiveness: Breaking the Power of the Past

Kay Arthur, David & BJ Lawson

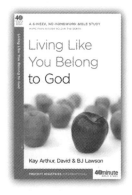

Living Like You Belong to God

Kay Arthur, David & BJ Lawson

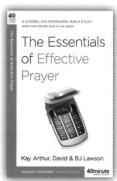

The Essentials of Effective Prayer

Kay Arthur, David & BJ Lawson

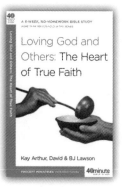

Loving God and Others: The Heart of True Faith

Kay Arthur, David & BJ Lawson

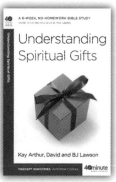

Understanding Spiritual Gifts

Kay Arthur, David and BJ Lawson

Also Available:
A Man's Strategy for Conquering Temptation
Rising to the Call of Leadership
Key Principles of Biblical Fasting
What Does the Bible Say About Sex?
Turning Your Heart Toward God
Fatal Distractions: Conquering Destructive Temptations
Spiritual Warfare: Overcoming the Enemy
The Power of Knowing God
Breaking Free from Fear

Another powerful study series
from beloved Bible teacher

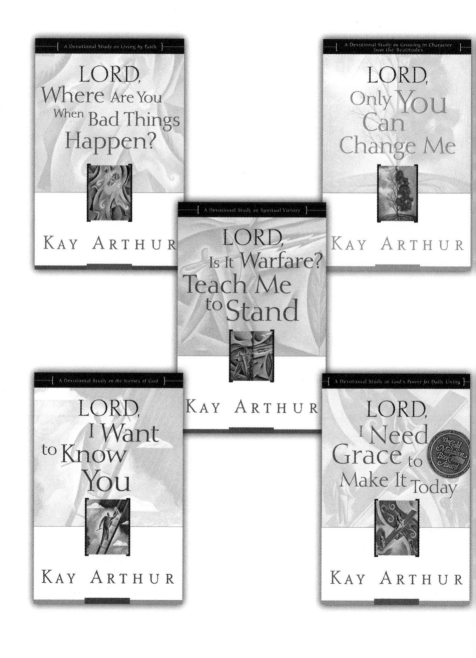

{ A Devotional Study on Living by Faith }

LORD,
Where Are You
When Bad Things
Happen?

KAY ARTHUR

{ A Devotional Study on Growing in Character from the Beatitudes }

LORD,
Only You
Can
Change Me

KAY ARTHUR

{ A Devotional Study on Spiritual Victory }

LORD,
Is It Warfare?
Teach Me
to Stand

KAY ARTHUR

{ A Devotional Study on the Names of God }

LORD,
I Want
to Know
You

KAY ARTHUR

{ A Devotional Study on God's Power for Daily Living }

LORD,
I Need
Grace to
Make It Today

The Gold Medallion Book Award

KAY ARTHUR

KAY ARTHUR

The Lord series provides insightful, warm-hearted Bible studies designed to meet you where you are—and help you discover God's answers to your deepest needs.

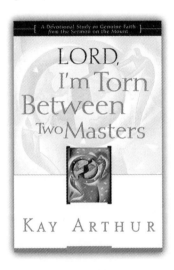

[A Devotional Study on Genuine Faith from the Sermon on the Mount]

LORD, I'm Torn Between Two Masters

KAY ARTHUR

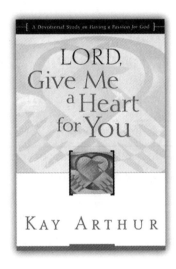

[A Devotional Study on Having a Passion for God]

LORD, Give Me a Heart for You

KAY ARTHUR

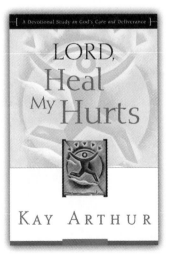

[A Devotional Study on God's Care and Deliverance]

LORD, Heal My Hurts

KAY ARTHUR

ALSO AVAILABLE:
One-year devotionals to draw you closer to the heart of God.

365 Appointments with God

Lord, I Give You This Day

KAY ARTHUR

365 APPOINTMENTS WITH GOD

SEARCH MY HEART, O GOD

KAY ARTHUR

ABOUT KAY ARTHUR AND PRECEPT MINISTRIES INTERNATIONAL

KAY ARTHUR is known around the world as an international Bible teacher, author, conference speaker, and host of the national radio and television programs *Precepts for Life,* which reaches a worldwide viewing audience of over 94 million. A four-time Gold Medallion Award–winning author, Kay has authored more than 100 books and Bible studies.

Kay and her husband, Jack, founded Precept Ministries International in 1970 in Chattanooga, Tennessee, with a vision to establish people in God's Word. Today, the ministry has a worldwide outreach. In addition to inductive study training workshops and thousands of small-group studies across America, PMI reaches nearly 150 countries with inductive Bible studies translated into nearly 70 languages, teaching people to discover Truth for themselves.

Contact Precept Ministries International for more information about inductive Bible studies in your area.

Precept Ministries International
PO Box 182218
Chattanooga, TN 37422-7218
800-763-8280
www.precept.org